TABLE OF CONTENTS

MEU (SOC): ANSWER TO THE MOST LIKELY THREAT
IN THE TWENTY-FIRST CENTURY

I. INTRODUCTION.

The balance of power in the world has shifted from a bipolar form, the United States and the

Soviet Union, to a multipolar orientation. Even though the United States is considered the only

remaining superpower, this does not mean that there is not a large threat to global stability. The

future threat will jeopardize stability through the medium of state fragmentation; conflicts will

not only be between states but within states. Causal factors will vary widely between cultural,

ethnic, political, and religious animosity, and other aggravating circumstances will include the

ravages of disease, overpopulation, crime, and resource depletion. The responsible actors in this

confused environment will not be easy to identify. Instead of a situation where there are good

guys and bad guys, the future actors will be gray guys; difficult to distinguish from the

population but just as deadly as any uniformly attired enemy soldier. Future conflicts will extend

between the most technologically advanced nation and the most basic agrarian society, and they

will occupy the spectrum separating conventional armed conflict and Operations Other Than

War (OOTW). The future threat will be multidimensional with a large pool of potential enemies.

The central components of the National Security Strategy of Engagement and Enlargement

(NSS) are reflective of the issues related above and they are intended to enhance the safety and

security of both the United States and the other regions of the world. These components are:

maintain a strong defense capability and promote cooperative security measures; work to open

foreign markets and spur global economic growth; and promote democracy abroad.[1] The future threat will require cooperative security measures because of the widespread nature of the threat base, and boosting global economic growth will serve to reduce the wide disparity between the haves and the have-nots. The promotion of democracy, with its focus on decreasing the level of instability present in a particular region, will enhance the safety of the entire global environment.

No single military service will be able to counter every aspect of the future threat, the nature of future operations will necessarily become more joint and combined in response to frequent and widely varied threats and crises. The key factor in this equation is to correctly anticipate the demands that the future threat will place on the military and then devise, or revise, the capabilities necessary to counter that threat. There must be a focus on forces that are ready to meet the challenges of the future; the tendency to build force structure consistent with the last war must be broken.

The question facing Marine Corps planners as the turn of the century rapidly approaches is whether the Marine Expeditionary Unit-Special Operations Capable (MEU (SOC)) program is an appropriate response to the challenges of the twenty-first century. This question is important as future Operations Other Than War (OOTW) threat scenarios will require new insights to match new challenges. The most likely future threat must be predicted, and credible counter-measures must be prepared to meet that threat. This work will focus on those countermeasures offered by the Marine Corps' MEU (SOC) program, and their strengths and shortcomings.

II. THE MOST LIKELY THREAT INTO THE TWENTY-FIRST CENTURY.

THE NATURE OF THE FUTURE THREAT

The essential nature of the future threat lies in the structure of the future global system. According to one scholar, this structure is "the single most important determinant of U.S.

national security strategy. It shapes how and why military force will be used. It determines who (or what) are the allies and the enemies. Roles and missions, force structure, training, equipment, and doctrine all depend on the structure of the future global system."[2] While it is impossible to determine the exact structure of this system, the ideas of the various authors described below yield an assessment of the threat challenges that will be posed against it.

Before the break up of the Soviet Union, nations were likely to be characterized by their political or economic systems and threat countries were identified by their affiliation to the Communist dogma. Samuel Huntington states that, "The great divisions among humankind and the dominating source of conflict will be cultural,"[3] a rift which has intensified since the end of the cold war. Culture and civilization are also included in another scholar, Robert Kaplan, and his view of the future threat: "…scarcity, crime, overpopulation, tribalism, and disease are rapidly destroying the social fabric of our planet."[4] Using events in West Africa he describes subcultures that transcend national boundaries and defy law and order. The combined vision of these two men presents a vision of the haves versus the have-nots.

The discussion of the attempt to define the essence of the future threat turns to broader concepts such as Low Intensity Conflict (LIC) being the preeminent threat against the technologically dominant nations of the Western world. One noted military historian, explains:

> In the future, war will not be waged by armies but by groups whom we today call terrorists, guerrillas, bandits, and robbers, but who will undoubtedly hit on more formal titles to describe themselves. Their organizations are likely to be constructed on charismatic lines rather than institutional ones, and to be motivated less by "professionalism" than by fanatical, ideologically-based, loyalties.[5]

This statement describes warfare between diverse factions in pursuit of equally diverse goals. Conflicts will arise between groups embracing differing ideologies, with the more advanced nations trying to counter their tactics with a superiority in technology-based systems.

The way we make wealth may be the way we make war. Other ideas regarding the future global system are based on three waves that make-up the civilizations of the world. In this paradigm: "the deepest economic and strategic change of all is the coming division of the world into three distinct, and potentially clashing civilizations....the first still symbolized by the hoe; the second by the assembly line; and the third by the computer."[6] Societies dependent on this scheme will be in constant competition with each other as they strive to move from a first wave economy to a third wave economy. This will drive the future threat and set the context in which most wars from now on will be fought.[7]

These ideas are linked in their use of technology and ideology as a basis for the future threat. Technology, and its offspring weapons and systems, becomes irrelevant when pitted against technologically inferior factions. For these inferior factions, if technology cannot be bought or developed, then non-technological counter-measures will be developed and employed which may even the playing field. On a more basic level, differences in the ideological make-up of societies will also foster the rise of many conflicts. The consensus of thinkers such as van Crevald, the Tofflers, Huntington and Kaplan is that the future threat will include a multidimensional threat base with an exceptionally large pool of potential enemies.

The National Security Strategy (NSS) of the United States, in turn, offers four principle dangers as the basis for the future threat: regional instability, the proliferation of weapons of mass destruction, transnational dangers, and dangers to democracy and reform.[8] The parallel between this document and the theories expressed above is striking. It is possible that, consciously or unconsciously, senior United States leaders are understanding the theories of scholars. This combination is a strong one, and offers optimism for understanding of the future threat.

To continue this discussion, ethnicity, ethnonationalism, and religious fundamentalism are the most frequently identified causes of regional instability and state fragmentation, because of their underlying ideological fervor.[9] The proliferation of Weapons of Mass Destruction (WMD) is a danger driven by technology; countries, or factions, that do not possess a strong technological base can obtain these weapons and use them against adversaries of much greater strength and power. The transnational dangers mentioned in the NSS are defined by drug trafficking and terrorism, and the subcultures that engage in these activities transcend national boundaries, they defy the laws of good order and discipline, and they serve to destabilize the global environment. Dangers to democracy and reform, is a broad category that encompasses threats against the community of democratic nations and free-market economies. The anticipated threat foreseen in the NSS, is that of a multidimensional threat base with any number of possible enemies.

The global environment and the potential threats that the United States will face in the twenty-first century will be significantly different from that of the Cold War era. Samuel Huntington, in an article about America's changing strategic interests, describes the future threat environment as having two characteristics, "First, the relations between countries may be more volatile and possibly more duplicitous than they were in the Cold War years....Second, relations among countries are likely to be more ambivalent; the world of 'good guys and bad guys' will give way to a world of 'gray guys.'"[10] Regardless of the structure of the future global system, the key point is that the multidimensional nature of this threat base, coupled with a staggering number of potential enemies, will pose a significant challenge to this nation's military forces.

WHO ARE THE MOST LIKELY THREAT ACTORS?

The enemies the United States will most likely face into the twenty-first century will not be soldiers in the traditional sense, but that they will be "warriors--erratic primitives of shifting allegiance, habituated to violence, with no stake in civil order. Unlike soldiers, warriors do not play by traditional rules, do not respect treaties, and do not obey orders they do not like."[11] In societies that are dominated by increasing levels of social breakdown, the enemy will reflect his environment making identification of the hostile participants a difficult task. The threat environment facing the United States into the twenty-first century will be shaped by the various actors and situations that influence worldwide events, and one key factor in understanding this phenomenon is making the distinction between warrior and soldier.

In recent years the visibility of groups such as tribesmen, mercenaries, terrorists, pirates, bandits, partisans, and gangs has been overshadowed by the focus on the Cold War tensions between the United States and the Soviet Union. These groups were held in check by the presence of Soviet troops or the strong influence of Soviet-backed governments, however one consequence of the diffusion of power at the end of the Twentieth Century has been the resurgence of the 'warrior'.[12]

One theory breaks down the origins of the warrior class into five categories in terms of their social and psychological origins.[13] The makeup of this new warrior class will vary from country to country and no two groups will be alike as they will emerge from a variety of sources. In general terms, distinctions between soldier and warrior may be charted as follows:

THE SOLDIER • THE WARRIOR

Sacrifice • Spoils
Disciplined • Semi or undisciplined
Organizational orientation • Individualist
Skills focus on defeating other soldiers • Skills focus directly on violence
Allegiance to state • Allegiance to charismatic figure, cause, or paymaster
Recognized legal status • Outside the law
"Restorer of order" • "Destroyer of order"[14]

These traits describe all warriors and show the threat facing the United States into the twenty-first century. Distinctions between soldier and warrior are crucial for understanding how America will function in worldwide events and in the new threat environment.

WHERE WILL THE MOST LIKELY THREAT BE ENCOUNTERED?

While an exact prediction is impossible, indicators narrow the future threat to the nations of the Third World and areas known as littoral regions as the cause of global instability. The term Third World, from one point of view, is a general reference to the lesser-developed nations of the world. Whether a country is deemed to be a third world country or not, depends on the terms of reference that are used to establish a particular level of cultural, economic, political, or social development. Rod Paschall, a military historian, frames the Third World as follows:

> Although esoteric classification schemes have been developed to differentiate between various categories of the globe's poorer nations, most people recognize the term Third World as referring to the 113 preindustrial nations located in the southern hemisphere and lower tier of the northern hemisphere. These states are unfortunately becoming increasingly authoritarian, armed, populated, poor, and engaged in conflict. The term *developing world* is no longer appropriate because about one-third of these countries are experiencing economic regression, their people growing hungrier and more destitute with each passing day.[15]

The exact number of Third World countries is not important, but the adjectives used to qualify them are crucial to identifying where the future threat will be encountered.

Paschall's generalizations about the future threat and Third World countries appear valid as *Authoritarian* regimes do not embrace the ideals of democracy; the populace does not determine their leaders through the voting process, and the result is a country ripe for revolutionary

insurgencies and the subsequent effects of political instability, subversion, and terrorism. The

depth to which Third World countries are *armed* is increasing; weapons fuel the insurgencies that

these countries are so susceptible to, and they serve to increase the use of force as a means to

gain political goals. Third World countries are also growing increasingly populated accounting

for strife, starvation, refugee problems and economic dislocations which further strain the

stability of these nations. While the Third World has approximately 75 percent of the world's

population, but only 25 percent of the globe's gross national product, the gap between those with

wealth and those without is widening.[16] *Poor* countries are subject to the transnational threats of

mass migrations, drugs, rising crime, and environmental degradation which when combined with

ethnic and religious rivalry increase the chances of being *engaged in conflict.*

Threat factors that plague underdeveloped countries have a spill-over effect onto the more

developed nations. The Third World will, therefore, become of immediate interest to developed

nations. For example:

> These relations are apt to produce a greater use of stability operations. The permanent
> members of the U.N. Security Council are all northern hemisphere nations, while the vast
> majority of conflicts occur in the southern hemisphere and lower tier of the northern
> hemisphere. Most of the permanent Security Council member states have clients and
> substantial financial investments in the south and the developed states are dependent to some
> degree on southern raw materials. There is, therefore, a northern interest in southern stability.
> Second, the growing movement to identify and expose human rights abuses is a northern-
> inspired 'phenomenon with its focus largely directed at southern miscreants….Additionally,
> the north is increasingly turning a deaf ear to Third World economic woes and pleas for
> assistance. One reason for northern displeasure is the growing evidence of huge fortunes
> amassed by Third World government officials and large-scale capital flight from the world's
> poorest nations, lands that are in desperate need of development funds. These factors argue
> for an increased northern proclivity to bring order to southern pockets of instability.[17]

Threat factors associated with the future threat are not based entirely on economic factors; but on a wide set of circumstances. The above argument is based largely on the economic interests of the more developed nations, and uses reverse logic to draft reasons why the more developed nations will benefit from the stabilization of the lesser-developed nations. This argument lends credence to the identification of the Third World as the environment where future threats will occur.

The littorals can be tied to future conflict in the following way:

> Traditionally, trouble erupts wherever things of great value exist to generate quarrels. Further, a look at the globe reveals that, with a few exceptions (such as the United States, where we made extraordinary investment in transportation infrastructure), the bulk of capital wealth, technological fabric, and urban population centers are located within 50 miles of seas and oceans. In fact, nearly half of the world's manmade assets are found within 20 miles of its beaches. These coastal regions--and the adjacent ocean areas out to 100 miles--constitute the zones called littorals.[18]

In an article concerning expeditionary warfare, Lt Gen Charles Wilhelm, USMC, explains that all the great crises of this century have occurred within the boundaries of the littoral regions and offers four facts supporting this contention:

- 70 percent of the planet is covered by water and over 80 percent of the world's nations are in the littorals.
- 7 of every 10 people on earth live within 200 miles of the sea.
- 4 of every 5 national capitals are located within the littorals.
- 125 cities with a population of over 1 million are located in the littorals, and within 10 years that number will rise to 300 cities.[19]

III. THE MARINE CORP'S DOCTRINAL RESPONSE TO THE MOST LIKELY THREAT.

The Low-Intensity Conflict (LIC), or Operations Other Than War (OOTW) threat that the United States will most likely face into the twenty-first century appears vague and undefined. One writer states, "The issues of war and peace have become so complex, ambiguous, and multidimensional that they generate a confusing array of views, interpretations and United States policy alternatives."[20] This environment, as described earlier in this paper, is characterized by frequent instances of instability, civil disturbances, drug trafficking, terrorism, subversion, insurgency, guerrilla warfare, surrogate wars, and other forms of low-level violence. In turn, the issues of human pain, disease, hunger, and privation further complicate this environment. Several doctrinal approaches have been developed to frame the military response to the most likely threat that the United States will face into the twenty-first century; these are described below.

Low Intensity Conflict (LIC) is a broad description of the type of warfare that will encompass the most likely future threat into the twenty-first century. Army Field Manual (FM) 100-20, defines LIC as:

> A political-military confrontation between contending states or groups below conventional war and above the routine, peaceful competition among states. It frequently involves protracted struggles of competing principles and ideologies. Low intensity conflict ranges from subversion to the use of armed force. It is waged by a combination of means, employing political, economic, informational, and military instruments. Low intensity conflicts are often localized, generally in the Third World, but contain regional and global security implications.[21]

This lengthy explanation is an attempt to categorize American military missions that resemble war at their upper limits, yet fall short of a situation of peace at their lower limits. A close approximation of the military missions inherent in LIC is shown in its four major operational categories: support for insurgencies and counterinsurgencies, combatting terrorism, peacekeeping operations, and peacetime contingency operations. These four categories cover the spectrum of anticipated conflicts that may extend between the most technologically advanced nation and the most basic agrarian society.

Low Intensity Conflict and Operations Other Than War are terms that are often interpreted differently among planners. While the semantics of these two terms are different, the challenge remains to accurately anticipate appropriate missions to be derived from the future threat. For purposes of this discussion LIC and OOTW will be used interchangeably, and both are appropriate to the anticipated twenty-first century threat.

Military Operations Other Than War (OOTW)[22] also denotes a set of military operations that correspond closely to the demands of the most likely future threat. OOTW, also accommodates environments short of war, but attempts to place a more appropriate name on the relevant circumstances of the anticipated operation than those framed in the definition of LIC; "less than war but not peace." The frequency of these operations, the forms that they take, and their duration may vary greatly as will the operational environments in which they would exist. Some missions would occur under peaceful conditions, while others might begin as peaceful operations and evolve into armed encounters, and still others could occur with hostile conditions prevailing throughout the operation. In an illustration of this diversity, Joint Publication (JPUB) 3-0 establishes eight types of OOTW that encompass a wide range of activities where the military instrument of national power is used for purposes other than the large scale combat operations that are usually associated with war.[23]

The Marine Corps, in Fleet Marine Force Manual (FMFM) 6, divides OOTW into two broad categories based on the general goals of the crisis in question, and it then delineates specific military operations for each category. The first category, Operations that Deter War and Resolve Conflict, are derived from threat environments where the antagonists have resorted to armed conflict, and these operations are pursued with the goal of returning the situation to a state of peace. By their nature, these operations are higher in risk and more likely to escalate in scale than the following category. The second category, Operations that Promote Peace, involve the use of military forces in peacetime and they pursue the goal of preventing armed conflict and maintaining United States influence in foreign lands[24] The Marine Corps' doctrinal base for OOTW is derived from the multidimensional nature of the future threat, and its focus spans between direct combat and civil assistance. This doctrinal base, coupled with other specific training directives, is the standard to which the MEU (SOC) currently trains.

IV. THE MEU (SOC) AS A CREDIBLE COUNTER-MEASURE TO THE MOST LIKELY FUTURE THREAT.

The United States Armed Forces are in their ninth year of drawdown and no single service will be able to offer the appropriate capabilities to handle all the future crises alone, they will require the capabilities of the entire force operating in a joint environment. As the military force structure adapts to this reality, the particular abilities of certain military branches begin to stand out from the rest. The Commandant of the Marine Corps presented his view on the Marine Corps' role in the twenty-first century as follows:

> The Corps will be recognized as the crisis response force of choice--a certain force in an uncertain world, and ever ready to project the power and influence of the United States from the sea to any foreign shore. Across the entire spectrum of scenarios, ranging from military attack against our Nation or its interests, to acts of political violence against Americans abroad, to those operations currently described as "Military Operations Other Than War," the Nation will have one thought: "Send in the Marines."[25]

These comments indicate that, while the Marine Corps can respond to a wide variety of challenges, its main contribution will be to project power and influence from the sea to any foreign shore. The implication is that the Marine Corps' primary response to the future threat will be the Marine Expeditionary Unit-Special Operations Capability.

This section will examine the MEU (SOC) as a credible counter-measure to the most likely future threat; a threat that will require a wide variety of military responses ranging from humanitarian assistance to full-scale military operations. This examination will focus on three

topics: the overall MEU (SOC) program and its capabilities, employment against the most likely

future threat, and shortfalls.

THE MEU (SOC) PROGRAM AND ITS CAPABILITIES.

Samuel Huntington's description of volatile, duplicitous, and ambivalent relations both between and among countries frames the characteristics of the most likely future threat environment and portends a military force that will be able to offer responses ranging between peace operations and the ability to overcome armed resistance. In a commentary concerning MEU (SOC) capabilities, BGen Zinni, USMC, stated that, "The MEU (SOC) provides the Unified Commanders in Chief (CINCs) with an effective means of dealing with the uncertainties of future threats, providing as it does a forward-deployed unit that is inherently balanced, sustainable, flexible, responsive, expandable, and credible."[26]

The MEU (SOC) is a *balanced* combined arms organization which is inherently *sustainable* as it brings its own organic capability to an operation -- carrying fifteen days worth of supply -- and for extended operations, it has its own sea-based supply link with the deployed Amphibious Ready Group (ARG).[27] *Flexibility* is gained in the wide variety of assets with which to maneuver from the sea to objective.[28] The forward deployed position, coupled with the over-the-horizon (OTH) capabilities, allows for a *responsive* force that has a short reaction time and a wide area of influence; these factors imply that the MEU (SOC) can be one of the first units to arrive on the scene of a crisis. In situations where extra units are needed, the MEU (SOC) can act to facilitate *expansion* of the force on the ground. The MEU (SOC), by possessing the requisite training and equipment, offers a *credible* force to carry out both conventional and special operations missions.[29]

A multidimensional threat base with a wide variety of potential enemies will require forces that can operate in a host of environments ranging from peace to armed conflict. The conventional and special operations capabilities of the MEU (SOC) offer just such a force that the CINC can employ in a wide variety of forward-presence and stability operations. The MEU (SOC) is a forward-deployed force with the assets and capabilities that can provide strategic and operational flexibility in a theater of employment, and it is on duty around the world, twenty-four hours a day, every day.

MEU (SOC) EMPLOYMENT AGAINST THE MOST LIKELY FUTURE THREAT.

The MEU (SOC) program offers a wide variety of crisis response, power projection, and force employment options when arrayed against, the challenges of the twenty-first century. These phrases, coupled with operational reach, set the stage for relating MEU (SOC) employment against the most likely future threat.

The qualities that make the Third World littorals part of the future threat will continue to necessitate a credible crisis response force. The notion that conflicts arise where things of great value exist to generate quarrels is reflected in Fleet Marine Force Manual 1-2 with the observation that, "all American embassies and most of the politico-economic centers of gravity in Third World countries are located in the cities, and seventy-five percent of these are within twenty-five miles of a coastline -- which places them within range of Marine amphibious capabilities."[30]

A rapid response capability for future crises exists within the forward-deployed forces of the MEU (SOC); it is not a force that must be created and then deployed for a particular crisis. A MEU (SOC) sails in international waters, it does not threaten any country's sovereignty, and it is readily available for short-notice employment if a situation should get out of hand. Credible force structure and a forward-deployed posture, make timely MEU (SOC) actions possible in crisis response.

The ability to place credible forces into a crisis area is a crucial element in combatting the future threat. The size of America's permanent overseas presence has decreased significantly in recent years, and while many nations enjoy the sense of security that United States military forces offer, few of these countries are willing to allow basing rights for those forces on their home soil. With respect to this dilemma, George Crist, former CINC United States Central Command, comments that, "A feasible and realistic solution is to shift to a 'power projection strategy.'...forces capable of quickly moving anywhere in the world where a regional crisis or impending conflict threatens an ally or American vital interests."[31] In crises that require large amounts of power to be projected ashore, the ability of each MEU (SOC) to act as an enabling force will be crucial. A force that can operate in an area of poor or degraded infrastructure, typical of the Third World littorals, will be able to establish the required facilities to receive follow-on forces. In essence, the MEU (SOC) will be able to forcibly open the door, and keep it open, so that reinforcements can arrive in a relatively secure environment.

The MEU (SOC) presents a wide variety of force employment options that may be arrayed against the future threat. The MEU (SOC) is both versatile and controllable, and it can be custom tailored to the crisis at hand because it deploys with all the organic combined arms assets necessary to achieve a wide range of missions. One possible model of force employment options is depicted in Appendix A; MEU (SOC) missions and capabilities as compared to the different types of OOTW. The common element in this model is the ability to make a forcible entry, in adverse conditions against a hostile opponent or environment.[32]

The last topic to be discussed in this attempt to relate MEU (SOC) employment against the most likely future threat is operational reach. To be effective against the future threat, the

MEU (SOC) must be able to reach and influence the places where that threat will be located. The Third World littorals -- the location of the future threat -- are well within the operational reach of the MEU (SOC).

The response to crises in the Third World littorals will increasingly depend on forces arriving from the sea. This method of response is rooted in both the anticipated threat location and the reduction of viable response options. In a June 1995 paper on *Expeditionary Warfare,* Lt Gen Wilhelm, USMC, offered the following comments.

> The challenges we face in the littorals are marked by increased crises, increased involvement, and steadily diminishing access--over 867 overseas bases have been closed, replaced, or reduced in the last 4 years. This decrease in forward presence, combined with the increase in littoral crises, requires that we concentrate on our ability to undertake expeditionary warfare."[33]

This forward presence, and the subsequent rapid crisis response capability, will come from the forward deployed Naval and Marine forces in a specific area.

The operational reach of the MEU (SOC) is enhanced by its self sustaining nature and its reduced reliance on local infrastructure. Operations in the Third World littorals will be conducted in areas that are likely to have a degraded, or possibly nonexistent, infrastructure for the support of deployed military forces.[34] Once introduced into a crisis area, a self-reliant force minimizes any further strain on an already degraded infrastructure while still accomplishing the mission at hand. A MEU (SOC), with air, ground, and logistics elements united under one command, operates within the same guidelines of doctrine, training, and standing operating procedures (SOP's), plus all of these elements use interoperable equipment.

The MEU (SOC) is the Marine Corps' primary response to the challenges of the future threat because it offers a wide variety of options in the areas of crisis response, power projection, and force employment; it provides the operational reach to be effective in the places where that the most likely threat will be located. While the MEU (SOC) is not the answer to every situation or crisis, it does offer a credible response to many of the anticipated threat scenarios in the Third World littorals.

MEU (SOC) SHORTFALLS WITH RESPECT TO THE MOST LIKELY FUTURE THREAT.

The MEU (SOC) cannot, in its current form, offer the appropriate capability for every future crisis. While it offers credible force and capabilities for employment against elements of the future threat, the MEU (SOC) program is not the single answer to all of these future challenges; this program is but one portion of the nation's rapid crisis response. Within the MEU (SOC) program there are three major areas that need enhancement in response to the challenges of the most likely future threat: civil affairs capabilities, MEU (SOC) structure, and strategic lift.

The civil affairs capability of the MEU (SOC) program is deficient in the areas of cultural awareness and governmental/non-governmental agency interaction. Cultural awareness can be increased by deploying additional Foreign Area Officers (FAO's) who are often able to shed light on the true causal factors of a crisis through their intimate familiarity with that area's culture, economy, political climate, and society. The most likely future threat in the Third World littorals may require the application of military power and the finesse of diplomacy in the resolution of crisis situations. To help alleviate some of the angst that these situations will generate, the relationship between the Department of State, various Humanitarian Relief Organizations (HRO's), and the forward-deployed commander needs to be fostered and improved.[35]

The second major shortfall area to be examined is the MEU (SOC) structure, especially the areas of intelligence, operational planning, and force integration. The demands for timely and accurate intelligence will increase with regard to the most likely future threat in the Third World littorals; the hardest information to find and the most in demand will most likely be HUMINT -- information from human sources.[36] The varied nature of enemy threat groups may not lend themselves to technological exploitation, and expanded use of HUMINT Exploitation Teams (HET's) within the MEU (SOC) may be required in order to gather intelligence on these groups. The demands placed on operational planning are beyond the current capabilities of the deployed MEU (SOC) structure. Additional planners are needed to increase interoperabiity and provide for more effective liaison teams during the conduct of long-range deliberate planning and crisis action planning.[37] Force Integration is lacking with respect to the integration of the Navy SEALS and the embarked Force Reconnaissance Direct Action Platoon. Currently these two units have only limited interaction during the training and work-up phase of the MEU (SOC) deployment and their combined integration and employment into an in-extremis hostage situation would be difficult and potentially disastrous.[38]

The final major shortfall area to be examined is strategic lift, or the availability of amphibious shipping. The slow modernization of the Navy's amphibious fleet is the 'Achilles heel' of the MEU (SOC) program and its' ability to respond to the future threat in the Third World littorals.[39] Inadequate amphibious shipping has numerous side effects such as a reduced ability to perform forward presence and rapid crisis response, and reductions in forward-deployed sustainability hampers the ability of the MEU (SOC) to maintain a viable enabling force on a hostile shore. Until amphibious shipping is enhanced, the MEU (SOC) program will continue to rely on innovative thinking to keep its units forward-deployed in the face of the future challenges.

V. CONCLUSION.

The most likely future threat to the United States into the twenty-first century will manifest itself through various multidimensional challenges to the stability and structure of the entire global system. Events will be shaped by an emergent class of warriors whose existence is spawned by the chaotic nature of their environment -- the most likely future threat environment -- the littoral regions of the Third World.

As one portion of the United States' military response to this threat, the MEU (SOC) provides a limited, yet sustainable, combined arms force that is rapidly deployable to any point in the Third World littorals. This force is timely in its response as it is already forward-deployed, and with its existing equipment, training, and SOP's it can reach inland to affect a wide range of potential crisis areas. The MEU (SOC) has the military capabilities to conduct forced entry operations onto a hostile shore, and once ashore, it can perform a wide variety of conventional and special maritime operations missions.

The same skills and equipment needed for conventional missions are also used in many of the OOTW missions that demand quick reaction in areas with limited infrastructure. Where additional forces are required, the MEU (SOC) can act as an enabling force for follow-on echelons of progressively larger MAGTF's or other joint/combined forces. Not reliant on overflight rights or overseas bases, the MEU (SOC) offers a "cheap" diplomatic alternative in cases where the introduction of force into a crisis area may be necessary. With the anticipated arrival of enhanced mobility assets -- the AAAV and the V-22 Osprey -- it will be able to fully execute the doctrine of OMFTS. The MEU (SOC) is a credible force alternative.

The MEU (SOC) program is appropriate to the most likely challenges of the twenty-first century. However, like all military programs, it frequently needs to be reexamined to ensure that it is indeed on the right track. As the future threat continues to evolve on its current course, or if it should take a markedly different shape, Marine Corps Planners must constantly reevaluate the viability of the MEU (SOC) as a credible counter-measure to those threats. The anonymous aphorism "We've done so much with so little for so long, that now we think we can do everything with nothing forever." is not applicable to the Marine Corps in response to the challenges of the future threat.

[1]   *National Security Strategy,* 2-3.

[2]   Steven Metz, "Transregional Security Concerns," in *World View: The 1995 Strategic Assessment from the Strategic Studies Institute,* ed. Earl H. Tilford, Jr., Monograph, Strategic Studies Institute (Carlisle Barracks, PA: February 1995), 6.

[3]   Samuel P. Huntington, "The Clash of Civilizations," *Foreign Affairs* (Summer 1993): 22.

[4]   Robert D. Kaplan, "The Coming Anarchy," *The Atlantic Monthly,* (February 1994): 44.

[5]   Martin van Crevald, *The Transformation of War, The Most Radical Reinterpretation of Armed Conflict Since Clausewitz* (New York: The Free Press, 1991), 197.

[6]   Alvin and Heidi Toffler, *War and Anti-War, Survival at the Dawn of the 21st Century* (Boston: Little, Brown, and Company, 1993), 18-21.

[7]   Toffler, 25.

[8]   *A National Security Strategy of Engagement and Enlargement* (Washington, D.C.: The White House, February 1995), i-iii.

[9]   J. Marlow Schmauder and Richard H. Shultz, Jr., "Emerging Regional Conflicts and U.S. Interests: Challenges and Responses in the 1990's," *Studies in Conflict and Terrorism* Vol. 17, No. 1 (1994): 1.

[10]   Samuel P. Huntington, "America's Changing Strategic Interests," *Survival* Vol. XXXIII, No.1 (January-February 1991): 6.

[11]   Ralph Peters, "The New Warrior Class," *Parameters* Vol. XIV, No. 2 (Summer 1994): 16.

[12]   Peters, "Winning Against Warriors," source unclear (22 July 1994): 1.

[13]   Peters, "The New Warrior Class," 17-19, and "Winning Against Warriors," 6-8.

[14]   Peters, "The New Warrior Class," 18.

[15]   Rod Paschall, *LIC 2010, Special Operations & Unconventional Warfare in the Next Century* (Washington, D.C.: Pergamon-Brassey's, 1990), 31-32.

[16]   Paschall, 33.

[17] Paschall, 132-133.

[18] Charles E. Myers, Jr., "Littoral Warfare: Back to the Future," *Proceedings* Vol. 116/11/1,053 (November 1990): 49.

[19] Lt Gen Charles E. Wilhelm, USMC, "Expeditionary Warfare," *Marine Corps Gazette* Vol.79, No. 6 (June 1995): 28.

[20] COL James B. Motley, USA (Ret), "U.S. Unconventional Conflict Policy and Strategy," *Military Review* Vol. LXX, No. 1 (January 1990): 3.

[21] Field Manual (FM) 100-20, *Military Operations in Low Intensity* Conflict," (Washington, D.C.: Department of the Army, 5 December 1990), 1-1.

[22] The phrase Military Operations Other Than War would typically be abbreviated with the acronym MOOTW. This acronym, and its definition, is in a state of flux within the Department of Defense establishment. MOOTW is used interchangeably with OOTW (Operations Other Than War). Neither term exists in the Department of Defense Dictionary of Military and Associated Terms. The acronym OOTW is used exclusively in this paper but it is considered to be synonymous with the acronym MOOTW.

[23] Joint Publication (JPUB) 3-0, *Doctrine for Joint Operations* (Washington, D.C.: Joint Chiefs of Staff, 1 February 1995), V-7.

[24] Fleet Marine Force Manual (FMFM) 6, *Ground Combat Operations* (Washington, D.C.: Headquarters, United States Marine Corps, 4 April 1995), 7-1 to 7-17.

[25] Gen Charles C. Krulak, USMC, "A Marine Corps for the 21st Century," *Marine Corps Gazette* Vol. 79, No. 8 (August 1995): 13.

[26] BGen Anthony C. Zinni, USMC, "Forward Presence and Stability Missions: The Marine Corps Perspective," *Marine Corps Gazette* Vol. 77, No. 3 (March 1993): 60.

[27] Maj James B. Laster, USMC, *The Marine Corps' Role In Joint Special Operations: Are We Elite Enough,* Masters Thesis (Quantico, VA: United States Marine Corps Command and Staff College, 1993), 4.

[28] A MEU (SOC) deploys with a variety of mobility assets that can be employed directly from the ship to the objective ashore. These include: the Amphibious Assault Vehicle (AAV), Rubber Raiding Craft (RRC), Helicopter assets (the CH-53E, the CH-46E, and the UH-1N), and Navy Landing Craft Air Cushion (LCAC's) and other landing craft (LCM-8's and LCU's).

[29]   Marine Corps Order (MCO) 3120.9, *Policy for Marine Expeditionary Unit (Special Operations Capable)* (Washington, D.C.: Headquarters, United States Marine Corps, 28 March 1994), 4-7.

[30]   Fleet Marine Force Manual (FMFM) 1-2, *The Role of the Marine Corps in National Defense* (Washington, D.C.: Headquarters, United States Marine Corps, 21 June 1991), 3-13.

[31]   Gen George B. Crist, USMC (Ret), "A U.S. Military Strategy for a Changing World," *Strategic Review* Vol. XVIII, No. 1 (Winter 1990): 17.

[32]   Trainor, 30.

[33]   Wilhelm, 28-29.

[34]   Wilhelm, 29.

[35]   Jonathan T. Dworken, "Restore Hope: Coordinating Relief Operations," *Joint Force Quarterly* No. 8 (Summer 1995): 19.

[36]   General John R. Galvin, USA, "Conflict in the Post-Cold War Era," in *Low-Intensity Conflict, Old Threats in a New World,* ed. Edwin G. Corr, and Stephen Sloan (Boulder: Westview Press, 1992), 69.

[37]   Lt Col Thomas W. Williams, USMC, "MEU (SOC): The Jewel in the Crown of Our Corps," *Marine Corps Gazette* Vol. 78, No. 3 (March 1994): 32.

[38]   Col Robert B. Blouse Jr., USMC, "Post-deployment Brief of the 11th MEU (SOC)," lecture presented at the Marine Corps University, Command and Staff College, Quantico, VA, on 22 January 1996.

[39]   Department of the Navy, *1992 Posture Statement* (Washington, D.C.: Department of the Navy, April 1992), 30.

APPENDIX A: MEU (SOC) Missions/Capabilities and the Types of OOTW

	Arms Control	Combatting Terrorism	DOD Support to Counter-Drug Ops	Nation Assistance	NEO	Civil Support Ops	Peace Ops	Support to Counter-Insurgency
-C4I	X	X	X	X	X	X	X	X
-Battle Area Ingress/Egress	X	X	X	X	X	X	X	X
-Locate and Fix Enemy	X	X	X		X		X	X
-Engage the Enemy	X	X	X		X		X	X
-Rapid Staff Planning	X	X	X		X	X	X	X
-Joint Force Interoperability	X	X	X	X	X	X	X	X
-Amphibious Raids	X	X	X		X			X
-NEO		X			X			X
-Show of Force Ops				X			X	X
-Reinforcement Ops				X		X	X	X
-Security Ops	X			X		X	X	X
-Joint/Combined Training/Instruction Teams		X	X	X				X
-HCA						X	X	X
-Tactical Deception Ops		X		X			X	X
-Fire Support Control	X	X		X			X	X
-Counter-Intelligence Ops	X	X	X	X	X		X	X
-ITG	X	X	X		X	X	X	X
-SIGINT/EW	X	X	X	X	X		X	X
-MOUT	X	X			X		X	X
-Airfield/Port/Other Key Facility Seizure	X				X		X	X
-CQB	X	X	X		X	X	X	X
-Specialized Demolition Ops								
-Clandestine Recon and Surveillance Ops	X	X	X	X	X		X	X
-MIO	X	X	X					
-GOPLAT		X						X
-Clandestine Recovery Ops	X				X			X
-TRAP		X	X				X	X
-IHR		X			X		X	X
-Direct Action	X	X	X				X	X

24

APPENDIX B: DEFINITIONS OF OPERATIONS OTHER THAN WAR (OOTW)

•Excerpts taken from Joint Publication 3-0 Doctrine for Joint Operations, V-7 to V-13.

1. Arms Control. The main purpose of arms control is to enhance national security. Although it may be viewed as a diplomatic mission, the military can play a vital role. For example, U.S. military personnel may be involved in verifying an arms control treaty; may seize Weapons of Mass Destruction (WMD); may escort authorized deliveries of weapons and other materials (such as enriched uranium) to preclude loss or unauthorized use of these assets; or may dismantle or destroy weapons with or without the consent of the host nation. All of these actions help reduce threats to regional stability.

2. Combatting Terrorism. These measures are both offensive (counter-terrorism) and defensive (anti-terrorism) in nature. The former typically occurs outside the territory of the United States, while the latter may occur anywhere in the world.

3. Department of Defense (DOD) Support to Counterdrug Operations. The anti-drug plans and programs of the DOD are an integral part of the National Drug Control Strategy (NDCS) and include detection and monitoring; support to cooperative foreign governments; support for interdiction; support to drug law enforcement agencies; internal drug prevention and treatment programs; research and development; and Command, Control, Computers, and Intelligence (C4I) support.

4. Nation Assistance. The main objective of nation assistance is to assist a host nation with internal programs to promote stability, develop sustainability, and establish institutions responsive to the needs of the people. Security assistance and foreign internal defense are the primary means of providing nation assistance.

a. Security Assistance refers to a group of programs that provide defense articles and services, including training to eligible foreign countries and international organizations that further U.S. national security objectives.

b. Foreign Internal Defense supports a host-nation's fight against lawlessness, subversion, and insurgency.

5. Noncombatant Evacuation Operations (NEOs). The purpose of NEOs is to safely and quickly remove civilian noncombatants from an area outside the United States where they are, or may be, threatened. Although NEOs are principally conducted for U.S. citizens, Armed Forces of the United States may also evacuate citizens from host, allied, or friendly nations if the National Command Authority (NCA) determines it to be in the best interest of the United States.

6. Other Civil Support Operations. These operations encompass the following;

a. World-wide humanitarian assistance: Includes disaster relief, support to displaced persons as well as humanitarian and civic assistance.

b. Military support to civil authorities: Includes U.S. domestic actions applicable to disaster-related civil emergencies and civil defense for attacks directed against the territory of the United States.

c. Military assistance for civil disturbances: Includes military support to U.S. domestic law enforcement agencies, protection of life and federal property, and prevention of disruptions to federal functions.

7. Peace Operations. This term encompasses three general areas that are not typically conducted in the United States;

a. Peacemaking or diplomatic actions.

b. Peacekeeping or noncombat military actions.

c. Peace Enforcement or coercive use of military force.

8. Support to Insurgencies. Insurgencies attempt to exploit actual or perceived governmental weaknesses, such as failure to maintain law and order; inability to respond adequately to disasters; overreaction to civil disturbances; or failure to meet economic, political, ethnic, or social expectations. Organizational structures for U.S. support to insurgencies can be overt, low visibility, clandestine, or covert. The U.S. military principally trains and advises insurgent forces in unconventional warfare tactics, techniques, and procedures.

APPENDIX C: MARINE EXPEDITIONARY UNIT (SPECIAL OPERATIONS CAPABLE)

CAPABILITIES

•Excerpts taken from **MCO** 3120.9, *Policy for MEU (SOC),* 4-8.

A. <u>**Conventional Capabilities:**</u>

1. <u>Command. Control. Communications. Computers and Intelligence (C4I)</u>. C4I is the integration of communications, computers and intelligence technologies and procedures into a functional, cohesive system to support the commander. C4I permits entry into national, theater, joint and combined systems to support all-source intelligence fusion, and to permit MEU rapid planning, decision, dissemination and execution.

2. <u>Battle Area Ingress/Egress</u>. The capability to enter and exit a battle area.

3. <u>Locate and Fix the Enemy</u>. The capability to locate and fix the enemy, involving finding and identifying enemy forces, maintaining surveillance once located, assessing the capabilities and intentions, and reporting these findings.

4. <u>Engage the Enemy</u>. The capability to engage, destroy, or capture the enemy in a rural or urban setting, in hostile environments, with minimized/controlled collateral damage.

5. <u>Rapid Staff Planning</u>. The capability to rapidly plan and be prepared to commence execution of operations within six (6) hours of receipt of the warning order/alert order. Commencement of operations is signified by the launch of forces by air and/or surface means. This may range from the insertion of reconnaissance and surveillance assets in support of the mission to the actual launch of an assault force. Rapid staff planning is a key to the MEU (SOC)s overall operational success.

6. <u>Joint Force Interoperability</u>. The MEU will normally be committed in conjunction with joint or combined task force (J/CTF) operations. Interoperability depends on compatible C4I equipment and standardized procedures while embracing common terminology and techniques.

7. <u>Amphibious Raids</u>. The capability to conduct amphibious raids via air and/or surface means from extended ranges in order to inflict loss or damage upon opposing forces, create diversion, capture and/or evacuate individuals and material by swift incursion into an objective area followed by a planned withdrawal. The amphibious raid is the primary operational focus for the forward-operating MEU (SOC)s.

8. <u>Non-combatant Evacuation Operations (NEOs)</u>. The capability to conduct NEOs by evacuating and protecting non-combatants in either a permissive or non-permissive environment. This capability includes the requirement to provide a security force, evacuation control center, recovery force, medical support, and transportation of evacuees.

9. <u>Show of Force Operations</u>. The capability includes amphibious demonstrations, presence of forces, or flyovers in support of U.S. interests.

10. <u>Reinforcement Operations</u>. The capability to reinforce U.S. (or designated Allied/friendly) forces by helicopter and/or surface means. This includes the capability to conduct relief-in-place or a passage of lines.

11. <u>Security Operations</u>. The capability to protect U.S. (or designated Allied/friendly nation) property and non-combatants. This includes establishing an integrated local security perimeter, screening for explosive devices, and providing personal protection to designated individuals.

12. <u>Joint/Combined Training/Instruction Teams</u>. The capability to provide training and assistance to foreign military forces permitted by U.S. law.

13. <u>Humanitarian and Civic Assistance</u>. To provide services such as medical and dental care, minor construction repair to civilian facilities, temporary assistance to local government, and assistance to counter the devastation caused by a manmade or natural disaster.

14. <u>Tactical Deception Operations</u>. The capability to design and implement tactical deception operations plans in order to deceive the enemy through electronic means, feints, demonstrations, and ruses which cause the enemy to react or fail to react in a manner which assists in the accomplishment of the overall mission.

15. <u>Fire Support Control</u>. The capability to control and coordinate naval surface fire, air support and ground fire support coordination measures for U.S. or designated Allied/friendly forces.

16. <u>Counterintelligence Operations</u>. The capability to protect the MEU (SOC) against espionage, sabotage, terrorism, and subversion by developing and providing information the commander can use to undertake countermeasures to protect his resources.

17. <u>Initial Terminal Guidance (ITG)</u>. The capability to establish and operate navigational, signal, and/or electronic devices for guiding helicopter and surface waves from a designated point to a landing zone or beach.

18. <u>Signal Intelligence/Electronic Warfare (SIGINT/EW) Operations</u>. The capability to conduct tactical SIGINT, limited ground-based EW, and communications security (COMSEC) monitoring and analysis in direct support of the MAGTF.

19. <u>Military Operations in Urban Terrain (MOUT)</u>. The capability to conduct military

operations in a built-up area.

20. <u>Airfield/Ports/Other Key Facilities Seizure</u>. The capability to secure an airfield, port, or other key facility in order to support MAGTF missions or to receive follow-on forces.

B. <u>Maritime Special Operations Capabilities:</u>

1. <u>Close Quarters Battle (COB)</u>. The capability to conduct direct action missions, employing CQB combat and dynamic assault tactics and techniques.

2. <u>Specialized Demolition Operations</u>. The capability to conduct specialized breaching; to employ specialized demolitions in support of other special operations. This includes an explosive entry capability to support CQB.

3. <u>Clandestine Reconnaissance and Surveillance</u>. The capability for entry into an objective area by air, surface, or subsurface means in order to perform information collection, target acquisition, and other intelligence collection tasks.

4. <u>Maritime Interdiction Operations (MIO)</u>. The capability to conduct MIO in support of Vessel Boarding, Search and Seizure (VBSS) operations during day or night on a cooperative, uncooperative, or hostile contact of interest.

5. <u>Gas and Oil Platform Operations (GOPLAT)</u>. The capability to conduct seizure and/or destruction of offshore gas and oil platforms.

6. <u>Clandestine Recovery Operations</u>. The capability to conduct clandestine extraction of personnel or sensitive items from enemy controlled areas.

7. <u>Tactical Recovery of Aircraft and/or Personnel (TRAP)</u>. The capability to conduct overland recovery of downed aircraft and personnel, aircraft sanitization, and provide advanced trauma-life support in a benign or hostile environment.

8. <u>In-Extremis Hostage Rescue (LHR)</u>. The capability to conduct recovery operations during an in-extremis situation by means of an emergency extraction of hostages and/or sensitive items from a non-permissive environment and expeditiously transport them to a designated safe haven. The IHR capability will only be employed when directed by appropriate authority and when dedicated national assets are unavailable.

9. <u>Direct Action (DA)</u>. The capability to conduct raid, ambush, or direct assault tactics; conduct standoff attacks by fire from air, ground, or maritime platforms; and provide terminal guidance for precision-guided munitions.

BIBLIOGRAPHY

Books

Brassey's Mershon Center. *American Defense Annual.* Washington, D.C.: Brassey's, 1995.

Galvin, GEN John R. "Conflict in the Post-Cold War Era." In *Low-Intensity Conflict, Old Threats in a New World.* Ed. Edwin G. Corr and Stephen Sloan, 60-70. Boulder: Westview Press, 1992.

Heckler, Richard Strozzi. *In Search of the Warrior Spirit.* Berkeley: North Atlantic Books, 1990.

Paschall, Rod. *LIC 2010, Special Operations & Unconventional Warfare in the Next Century.* Washington, D.C.: Pergamon-Brassey's, 1990.

Peters, Ralph. *The War in 2020.* New York: Simon & Schuster, 1991.

Toffler, Alvin and Heidi. *War and Anti-War, Survival at the Dawn of the 21st Century.* Boston: Little, Brown, and Company, 1993.

van Crevald, Martin. *The Transformation of War.* New York: The Free Press, 1991.

Government Publications

A National Security Strategy of Engagement and Enlargement. Washington, D.C.: The White House. February 1995.

Department of the Navy, *1992 Posture Statement.* Washington, D.C.: Department of the Navy. April 1992.

Field Manual (FM) 7-98. *Operations in a Low-Intensity Conflict.* Washington, D.C.: Department of the Army. 19 October 1992.

Field Manual (FM) 33-1. *Psychological Operations.* Washington, D.C.: Department of the Army. 18February1993.

Field Manual (FM) 90-8. *Counterguerilla Operations.* Washington, D.C.: Department of the Army. August 1986.

Field Manual (FM) 100-19. *Domestic Support Operations.* Washington, D.C.: Department of the Army. July 1993.

Field Manual (FM) 100-20. *Military Operations in Low Intensity Conflict.* Washington, D.C.: Department of the Army. 5 December 1990.

Field Manual (FM) 100-23. *Peace Operations.* Washington, D.C.: Department of the Army. December 1994.

Fleet Marine Force Manual (FMFM) 1-2. *The Role of the Marine Corps in National Defense.* Washington, D.C.: United States Marine Corps. 21 June 191.

Fleet Marine Force Manual (FMFM) 6. *Ground Combat Operations.* Washington, D.C.: United States Marine Corps. 4 April 1995.

Fleet Marine Force Manual (FMFM) 7-14. *Combating Terrorism.* Washington, D.C.: United States Marine Corps. 5 October 1990.

Fleet Marine Force Manual (FMFM) 8-1. *Special Operations.* Washington, D.C.: United States Marine Corps. 8 May 1984.

Fleet Marine Force Manual (FMFM) 8-2. *Counterinsurgency Operations.* Washington, D.C.: United States Marine Corps. 29 January 1980.

Joint Publication (JPUB) 1-02. *Department of Defense Dictionary of Military and Associated Terms.* Washington, D.C.: Joint Chiefs of Staff. 1 December 1989.

Joint Publication (JPUB) 3-0. *Doctrine for Joint Operations.* Washington, D.C.: Joint Chiefs of Staff. 1 February 1995.

Joint Publication (JPUB) 3-05. *Doctrine for Joint Special Operations.* Washington, D.C.: Joint Chiefs of Staff. 28 October 1992.

Joint Publication (JPUB) TEST PUBLICATION 3-07. *Doctrine for Joint Operations in Low-Intensity Conflict.* Washington, D.C.: Joint Chiefs of Staff. August 1990.

Joint Publication (JPUB) 3-07.1. *Joint Tactics, Techniques, and Procedures for Foreign Internal Defense.* Washington, D.C.: Joint Chiefs of Staff. 20 December 1993.

Joint Publication (JPUB) 3-07.2. *Joint Tactics, Techniques, and Procedures for Antiterrorism.* Washington, D.C.: Joint Chiefs of Staff. 25 June 1993.

Joint Publication (JPUB) 3-07.3. *Joint Tactics, Techniques, and Procedures for Peacekeeping Operations.* Washington, D.C.: Joint Chiefs of Staff 29 April 1994.

Joint Task Force Commander's Handbook for Peace Operations. Fort Monroe, VA: Joint Warfighting Center. 28 February 1995.

Marine Corps Long-Range Plan (MLRP) 2000-2020. Washington, D.C.: Headquarters, United States Marine Corps. 28 June 1991.

Marine Corps Order (MCO) 3120.8A. *Policy for the Organization of Fleet Marine Forces for Combat.* Washington, D.C.: United States Marine Corps. 26 June 1992.

Marine Corps Order (MCO) 3120.9. *Policy for Marine Expeditionary Unit (Special Operations Capable).* Washington, D.C.: United States Marine Corps. 28 March 1994.

Report on the Bottom-Up Review. Washington, D.C.: Department of Defense. 21 October 1993.

Threats in Transition, Marine Corps Mid-Range Threat Estimate, 1995-2005. Quantico, VA: Marine Corps Intelligence Activity. November 1994.

White Paper. *Intelligence Support to Operations Other Than War.* Washington, D.C.: Office of the Assistant Secretary of Defense, Special Operations and Low Intensity Conflict. January 1994.

White Paper. *Operational Maneuver from the Sea.* Washington, D.C.: Headquarters, United States Marine Corps. 1995.

Lectures

Blouse, Col Robert B., Jr., USMC. "Post-deployment Brief of the 11th MEU (SOC)." Lecture presented at the Marine Corps University, Command and Staff College. Quantico, VA, 22 January 1996.

Monographs

Mazarr, Michael. *The Revolution in Military Affairs: A Framework for Defense Planning.* Strategic Studies Institute. Carlisle Barracks, PA: 10 June 1994.

Metz, Steven. "Transregional Security Concerns," in *World View: The 1995 Strategic Assessment from the Strategic Studies Institute.* Strategic Studies Institute. Carlisle Barracks, PA: February 1995.

Sullivan, GEN Gordon R., USA. *Land Warfare in the 21st Century.* Strategic Studies Institute. Carlisle Barracks, PA: February 1993.

Periodicals

Anderson, Col Gary W., USMC. "Campaign Planning for Operations Other Than War." *Marine Corps Gazette* Vol. 80, No. 2 (February 1996): 45-47.

Armitage, Richard L. "U.S. Security in the Pacific in the 21st Century." *Strategic Review* Vol. XVIII, No. 3 (Summer 1990): 9-18.

Armstrong, Lt Col Charles L., USMC. "Blueprint for the 1990's---Reengineering the Military Establishment." *Marine Corps Gazette* Vol. 77, No. 3 (March 1993): 50-55.

_____. "From Utility to Insanity---A Brief Overview of United Nations Failures." *Marine Corps Gazette* Vol. 78, No. 9 (September 1994): 46-48.

Arnold, S.L. and David T. Stahl. "A Power Projection Army in Operations Other Than War." *Parameters* Vol. XXIII, No. 4 (Winter 1993-94): 4-26.

Baker, Pauline H. and John A. Ausink. "State Collapse and Ethnic Violence: Toward a Predictive Model." *Parameters* Vol. XXVI, No. 1 (Spring 1996): 19-31.

Barber, CAPT Arthur H., III, USN. "Engagement through Deployment: Shaping America's Future Military." *Parameters* Vol. XXIV, No. 4 (Winter 1994-95): 19-29.

Barnes, COL Rudolph, Jr., USA. "Civil Affairs: Diplomat-Warriors in Contemporary Conflicts." *Special Warfare* Vol. 4, No. 1 (Winter 1991): 4-11.

Bateman, CPT Robert L., USA. "Force XXI and the Death of Auftragstaktik." *Armor* Vol. CV, No. 1 (January-February 1996): 13-15.

Bean, Maj Mark H., USMC. "Fourth Generation Warfare." *Marine Corps Gazette* Vol. 79, No. 3 (March 1995): 53-55.

Belbutowski, Paul M. "Strategic Implications of Cultures in Conflict." *Parameters* Vol. XXVI, No. 1 (Spring 1996): 32-42.

Blackwell, LTG Paul E., USA. "Winning the Wars of the 21st Century." *Army* Vol. 44, No. 10 (October 1994): 121-134.

Bolgiano, CPT David G., USA. "Firearms Training Systems: A Proposal for Future Rules of Engagement Training." *The Army Lawyer* (December 1995): 79-81.

Bowdish, LCDR Randall G., USN. "The Revolution in Military Affairs: The Sixth Generation." *Military Review* Vol. LXXV, No. 6 (November-December 1995): 26-33.

Boyd, BG Morris J., USA. "Peace Operations: A Capstone Doctrine." *Military Review* Vol. LXXV, No. 3 (May-June 1995): 20-29.

Bunker, Robert J. "Rethinking OOTW." *Military Review* Vol. LXXV, No. 6 (November-December 1995): 34-41.

_____. "The Transition to Fourth Epoch War." *Marine Corps Gazette* Vol. 78, No. 9 (September 1994): 20-32.

Chase, Col Eric L., USMC. "Summing up Roles and Missions: A Marine Corps Perspective." *Marine Corps Gazette* Vol. 79, No. 7 (July 1995): 60-67.

Crist, Gen George B., USMC (Ret). "A U.S. Military Strategy for a Changing World." *Strategic Review* Vol. XVIII, No. 1 (Winter 1990): 16-24.

Doherty, Terry. "FID in the 90's." *Special Warfare* Vol. 5, No. 1 (March 1992): 39-41.

Downie, Richard D. "Low-Intensity Conflict Doctrine and Policy: Old Wine in a New Bottle?" *Studies in Conflict and Terrorism* Vol. 15, No. 1 (January-March 1991): 53-67.

Dworken, Jonathan T. "Restore Hope: Coordinating Relief Operations." *Joint Force Quarterly* No. 8 (Summer 1995): 14-20.

Fenton, Lt Col George P., USMC. "Marine Expeditionary Units--On the Operational Level in MOOTW." *Marine Corps Gazette* Vol. 80, No. 3 (March 1996): 58-65.

Fitz-Simons, Daniel W. "Set and Drift, The Role of the Marine Corps over the Next Decade." *Naval War College Review* Vol. XLVI, No. 1, Sequence 341 (Winter 1993): 109-112.

Fromm, MAJ Peter, USA. "War and OOTW, Philosophical Foundations." *Military Review* Vol. LXXVI, No. 5 (September-October 1995): 57-62.

Gregson, Col Wallace C., Jr., USMC. "Sea-Based Indirect Warfare." *Marine Corps Gazette* Vol. 73, No. 5 (May 1990): 39-41.

Hammes, Lt Col Thomas X., USMC. "The Evolution of War: The Fourth Generation." *Marine Corps Gazette* Vol. 78, No. 9 (September 1994): 35-44.

Hanke, James S. and John H. Crerar. "Shifting Threat Moves Toward Lower Intensity Conflicts." *Signal* Vol. 45, No. 4 (December 1990): 21-26.

Hayden, Lt Col H.T., USMC. "Sounds of Battle Around the World." *Marine Corps Gazette* Vol. 77, No. 3 (March 1993): 62-71.

Hoffman, Maj F. G., USMC. "Preserving World Order With Naval Power." *Marine Corps Gazette* Vol. 80, No. 3 (March 1996): 36-37.

Hoffman, Michael H. "War, Peace, and International Armed Conflict: Solving the Peace Enforcer's Paradox." *Parameters* Vol. XXV, No. 4 (Winter 1995-1996): 41-52.

Huening, CPT Tim, USA, and CPT John A. Nagl. "Training a Divisional Cavalry Squadron for Operations Other Than War." *Armor* Vol. CV, No. 1 (January-February 1991): 23-24.

Hunter, COL Horace L., USA. "Ethnic Conflict and Operations Other Than War." *Military Review* Vol. LXXIII, No. 11 (November 1993): 18-24.

Huntington, Samuel P. "America's Changing Strategic Interests." *Survival* Vol. XXXIII, No. 1 (January-February 1991): 3-17.

_____. "The Clash of Civilizations." *Foreign Affairs* (Summer 1993): 22-49.

Hurley, Maj David W., USMC. "LIC---The Cultural Component." *Marine Corps Gazette* Vol. 73, No. 12 (December 1989): 19.

Jandora, John W. "Threat Parameters for Operations Other than War." *Parameters* Vol. XXV, No. I (Spring 1995): 55-67.

Kaplan, Robert D. "The Coming Anarchy." *The Atlantic Monthly* (February 1994): 44-76.

Kennedy, Paul. "Preparing for the 21st Century: Winners and Losers." *The New York Review* Vol. 40(11 February 1993): 32-44.

Kime, Capt Carl M., USMC. "Peacekeeping Operations: Maintaining "Consent" at the Tactical Level." *Marine Corps Gazette* Vol. 80, No. 2 (February 1996): 48-49.

Krulak, Gen Charles C., USMC. "A Marine Corps for the 21st Century." *Marine Corps Gazette* Vol. 79, No. 8 (August 1995): 12-13.

Lance, Maj Victor D., USMC. "MAGTF (SOC): Time to Make it Happen." *Marine Corps Gazette* Vol. 76, No. 7 (July 1992): 55-61.

Lasswell, James A. "Presence---Do We Stay or Do We Go?" *Joint Force Quarterly* No. 8 (Summer 1995): 83-85.

Lind, William S., Maj John F. Schmitt, USMCR, and Col Gary I. Wilson, USMCR. "Fourth Generation Warfare: Another Look." *Marine Corps Gazette* Vol. 78, No. 12 (December 1994): 34-37.

Lind, William S., Col Keith F. Nightengale, USMC, Capt John F. Schmitt, USMCR, Col Joseph W. Sutton, USMC, and Lt Col Gary I. Wilson, USMCR. "The Changing Face of War: Into the Fourth Generation." *Marine Corps Gazette* Vol. 73, No. 10 (October 1989): 22-26.

Linn, Maj Thomas C., USMC. "Debating Marine Corps Roles and Missions." *Marine Corps Gazette* Vol. 79, No. 3 (March 1995): 84-88.

_____. "MAGTF Capabilities in an Uncertain World." *Marine Corps Gazette* Vol. 73, No. 5 (May 1990), 33-37.

Mann, Steven R. "Chaos Theory and Strategic Thought." *Parameters* Vol. XXII, No. 3 (Autumn 1992): 54-68.

McKenzie, Kenneth F. "Elegant Irrelevance: Fourth Generation Warfare." *Parameters* Vol. XXIII, No. 3 (Autumn 1993): 51-60.

_____. "The Marine Corps Of Tomorrow." *Proceedings* Vol. 119/11/1,089 (November 1993): 28-31.

Metz, Steven. "A Flame Kept Burning: Counterinsurgency Support After the Cold War." *Parameters* Vol. XXV, No. 3 (Autumn 1995): 31-40.

_____. "U.S. Strategy and the Changing LIC Threat." *Military Review* Vol. LXXI, No. 6 (June 1991): 22-29.

Moore, Maj R. Scott, USMC. "Looking Back at the Future: The Practice and Patterns of Expeditionary Operations in the 20th Century." *Marine Corps Gazette* Vol. 77, No. 8 (August 1993): 72-77.

_____. "Small War Lessons Learned." *Marine Corps Gazette* Vol. 77, No. 2 (February 1993): 32-36.

Morris, CPT Tamara L., USA. "The IPB Process for Operations Other Than War." *Field Artillery* (September-October 1995): 28-31.

Morrison, Philip, Kosta Tsipis, and Jerome Wiesner. "The Future of American Defense." *Scientific American* Vol. 270, No. 2 (February 1994): 38-47

Motley, COL James B., USA (Ret). "U.S. Unconventional Conflict Policy and Strategy." *Military Review* Vol. LXX, No. 1 (January 1990): 2-16.

Mundy, Gen Carl E., Jr., USMC. "Redefining the Marine Corps' Strategic Concept." *Proceedings* Vol. 118/5/1,071 (May 1992): 66-70.

Myers, Charles E., Jr. "Littoral Warfare: Back to the Future." *Proceedings* Vol. 116/11/1,053 (November 1990): 48-55.

Peters, Ralph. "Our Soldiers, Their Cities." *Parameters* Vol. XXVI, No. 1 (Spring 1996): 43-50.

_____. "The Culture of Future Conflict." *Parameters* Vol. XXV, No. 4 (Winter 1995-96): 18-27.

_____. "The Movable Fortress: Warfare in the 21st Century." *Military Review* Vol. LXXIII, No. 6 (June 1993): 62-72.

_____. "The New Warrior Class." *Parameters* Vol. XIV, No. 2 (Summer 1994): 16-26.

_____."Vanity and the Bonfires of the "isms"." *Parameters* Vol. XXIII, No. 3 (Autumn 1993): 39-50.

Prina, Edgar. "The CINC's Testify on New World Order." *Sea Power* Vol. 34, No. 7 (July 1991): 35-39.

Quinlivan, James T. "Force Requirements in Stability Operations." *Parameters* Vol. XXV, No. 4 (Winter 1995-1996): 59-69.

Quist, Col Burton C., USMC. "Naval Expeditionary Warfare Update." *Marine Corps Gazette* Vol. 80, No. 3 (March 1996): 38-41.

Record, Jeffrey. "Ready for What and Modernized Against Whom? A Strategic Perspective on Readiness and Modernization." *Parameters* Vol. XXV, No. 3 (Autumn 1995): 31-40.

Rylander, Lynn R. "The Future of the Marines in Small Wars." *Naval War College Review* Vol. XL, No. 4/Sequence 320 (Autumn 1987): 64-75.

Schmauder, J. Marlow, and Richard H. Shultz, Jr. "Emerging Regional Conflicts and U.S. Interests:Challenges and Responses in the 1990's." *Studies in Conflict and Terrorism* Vol. 17, No. 1(1994): 1-21.

Siegel, Adam B. "It's Nothing New." *Marine Corps Gazette* Vol. 79, No. 11 (November 1995): 48.

Smith, Maj Brantley O., USMC. "The Red Cross With Guns (or, Using Warriors as Relief Workers)." *Marine Corps Gazette* Vol. 77, No. 10 (October 1993): 12-16.

Sood, V.K. "Low-Intensity Conflict: The Source of Third-World Instability." *Studies in Conflict and Terrorism* Vol. 15, No. 4 (October-December 1992): 233-250.

Stoft, William A., and Gary L. Guertner. "Ethnic Conflict: The Perils of Military Intervention." *Parameters* Vol. XXV, No. 1 (Spring 1995): 30-42.

Story, Ann E., and Aryea Gottlieb. "Beyond the Range of Military Operations." *Joint Force Quarterly* No. 9 (Autumn 1995): 99-104.

Stringer, Capt Kevin D., USMC. "The MAGTF in OOTW." *Marine Corps Gazette* Vol. 79, No. 11 (November 1995): 53-54.

Szafranski, Richard. "Thinking About Small Wars." *Parameters* Vol. XX, No. 3 (September 1990): 39-49.

_____. "When Waves Collide: Future Conflict." *Joint Force Quarterly* No. 7 (Spring 1995): 77-84.

Tangredi, LCDR Sam J., USN. "Pacific Garrison or Contingency Force? Implications of the New National Security Strategy for the Marine Corps." *Naval War College Review* Vol. XLV, No. 3, Sequence 339 (Summer 1992): 13-20.

Trainor, Lt Gen Bernard E., USMC (Ret). "A Force 'Employment' Capability." *Marine Corps Gazette* Vol. 73, No. 5 (May 1990): 27-3 1.

_____. "Unconventional Warfare." *Marine Corps Gazette* Vol. 73, No. 10 (October 1989): 16-21.

Turbiville, Graham H. "Operations Other Than War: Organized Crime Dimension." *Military Review* Vol. LXXIV, No. 1 (January 1994): 35-47.

_____ "Operations Other Than War in the Asia-Pacific Theater." *Military Review* Vol. LXXIV, No. 4 (April 1994): 20-21.

van Crevald, Martin. "The Fate of the State." *Parameters* Vol. XXVI, No. 1 (Spring 1996): 4-18.

Weltsch, Maj Michael D., USMC. "Nationbuilding and the Marine Corps." *Marine Corps Gazette* Vol. 77, No. 2 (February 1993): 30-32.

Wilhelm, Lt Gen Charles E., USMC. "Expeditionary Warfare." *Marine Corps Gazette* Vol. 79, No. 6 (June 1995): 28-30.

Williams, Lt Col Thomas W., USMC. "MEU (SOC): The Jewel in the Crown of Our Corps." *Marine Corps Gazette* Vol. 78, No. 3 (March 1994): 30-32.

Wyly, Col Michael D., USMC. "Fourth Generation Warfare: What Does It Mean to Every Marine?" *Marine Corps Gazette* Vol. 79, No. 3 (March 1995): 55-56.

Yost, David S. "The Future of U.S. Overseas Presence." *Joint Force Quarterly* No. 8 (Summer 1995): 70-82.

Young, Lewis P. "The USMC---The Search For a Post-Cold War Role And a Means to Ensure Funding." *Asian Defence Journal* (June 1993): 18-23.

Zinni, BGen Anthony C., USMC. "Forward Presence and Stability Missions: The Marine Corps Perspective." *Marine Corps Gazette* Vol. 77, No. 3 (March 1993): 56-61.

Unpublished Theses

Cash, Maj Steven J., USMC. *Marine Expeditionary Units in the 1990's.* Masters Thesis. Newport, RI: Naval War College, 1992.

Clemmer, Lt Col Wayne A., USMC. *Low-Intensity Conflicts and the United States Marine Corps.* Final Study Report. Carlisle Barracks, PA: United States Army War College, 5 April 1991.

Foersch, Maj Warren J., USMC. *Preparations Still Needed for the 21st Century.* Military Issues Paper. Quantico, VA: United States Marine Corps Command and Staff College, 1994.

Kirkley, Maj C.E., USMC. *Low-Intensity Conflict and the Marine Air-Ground Task Force.* Military Issues Paper. Quantico, VA: United States Marine Corps Command and Staff College, 1992.

Laster, Maj James B., USMC. *The Marine Corps' Role In Joint Special Operations: Are We Elite Enough?* Masters Thesis. Quantico, VA: United States Marine Corps Command and Staff College, 1993.

Miller, Maj Walter L., Jr., USMC. *Operations Other Than War: Where Are We Heading?* Military Issues Paper. Quantico, VA: United States Marine Corps Command and Staff College, 1994-95.

Murphy, LCDR Frank J., USN. *Littoral Warfare: Adapting to Brown-Water Operations.* Military Issues Paper. Quantico, VA: United States Marine Corps Command and Staff College, 1993.

Nicholson, Maj Lawrence D., USMC. *An Analysis of the Twenty-One Missions of the Marine Corps Expeditionary Unit (Special Operations Capable).* Masters Thesis. Fort Leavenworth, KS: United States Command and General Staff College, 1994

Parrish, Lt Col W. H., USMC. *CINCSOUTH's Ounce of Prevention or Pound of Cure -The Marine Expeditionary Unit (MEU).* Masters Thesis. Newport, RI: Naval War College, 14 May 1990.

Smith, Maj Brantley O., USMC. *The Red Cross With Guns (or. Using Warriors as Relief Workers).* Military Issues Paper, Quantico, VA: United States Marine Corps Command and Staff College, 1993.

Wood, Maj Mark F., USMC. *Marine Expeditionary Unit Special Operations Capable.* Military Information Paper. Quantico, VA: United States Marine Corps Command and Staff College, 27 February 1995.